PRESIDENTS' DAY

by Charly Haley

Cody Koala

An Imprint of Pop!
popbooksonline.com

abdobooks.com

Published by Pop!, a division of ABDO, PO Box 398166, Minneapolis, Minnesota 55439. Copyright © 2019 by POP, LLC. International copyrights reserved in all countries. No part of this book may be reproduced in any form without written permission from the publisher. Pop!™ is a trademark and logo of POP, LLC.

Printed in the United States of America, North Mankato, Minnesota

082018
012019

THIS BOOK CONTAINS RECYCLED MATERIALS

Cover Photo: iStockphoto
Interior Photos: iStockphoto, 1, 17; Shutterstock Images, 5 (top), 5 (bottom left), 5 (bottom right), 7, 9, 10, 13, 15, 18, 20, 21

Editor: Meg Gaertner
Series Designer: Laura Mitchell

Library of Congress Control Number: 2018949239

Publisher's Cataloging-in-Publication Data

Names: Haley, Charly, author.
Title: Presidents' day / by Charly Haley.
Description: Minneapolis, Minnesota : Pop!, 2019 | Series: Holidays | Includes online resources and index.
Identifiers: ISBN 9781532161988 (lib. bdg.) | ISBN 9781641855693 (pbk) | ISBN 9781532163043 (ebook)
Subjects: LCSH: Presidents' day--Juvenile literature. | Holidays--Juvenile literature. | Washington-Lincoln Day--Juvenile literature.
Classification: DDC 394.261--dc23

Hello! My name is

Cody Koala

Pop open this book and you'll find QR codes like this one, loaded with information, so you can learn even more!

Scan this code* and others like it while you read, or visit the website below to make this book pop.

popbooksonline.com/presidents-day

*Scanning QR codes requires a web-enabled smart device with a QR code reader app and a camera.

Table of Contents

Chapter 1

Presidents' Day

People show American flags. They talk about presidents at school. It is Presidents' Day.

Watch a video here!

Presidents' Day is celebrated the third Monday of February. People honor former presidents George Washington and Abraham Lincoln. Some people celebrate all presidents on the holiday.

Washington and Lincoln had birthdays in February.

February

Mon	Tue	Wed	Thu	Fri	Sat	Sun
						1
2	3	4	5	6	7	8
9	10	11	(12)	13	14	15
(16)	17	18	19	20	21	(22)
23	24	25	26	27	28	

16

Presidents' Day

12

Lincoln's birthday

22

Washington's birthday

Chapter 2

George Washington

Presidents' Day was created in the 1880s. It was meant to **honor** George Washington. He was the first president of the United States.

Learn more here!

Washington was a leader during the **American Revolutionary War**. He led the American army against Great Britain. The Americans won the war. The United States became a country.

Chapter 3

Abraham Lincoln

Presidents' Day was moved in the 1970s. **Government** leaders changed the date. They wanted to honor Abraham Lincoln, too.

Learn more here!

Lincoln was president during the American Civil War. At that time, white people held black people as slaves. Lincoln worked to make slavery illegal. Eventually, all slaves were freed.

Chapter 4

Celebrations

Presidents' Day is often celebrated with community events. People may talk about the presidents. They may celebrate the things they love about the United States.

Complete an
activity here!

In some countries, people must celebrate government holidays. But in the United States, people have the right to choose. They do not have to celebrate Presidents' Day.

Some people
might not celebrate if
they are unhappy with
the government.

Washington and Lincoln
worked to give people
that choice.

Lincoln was the
16th president of the
United States.

Making Connections

Text-to-Self

Have you ever celebrated Presidents' Day?
How would you like to celebrate it?

Text-to-Text

Have you read any other books about holidays?
What did you learn?

Text-to-World

Presidents' Day celebrates two former presidents.
What other former or current presidents have you
heard mentioned in the news?

Glossary

American Civil War – a war in the 1860s between the North and South of the United States.

American Revolutionary War – a war in the late 1700s between Great Britain and Americans.

government – the people who run a country.

honor – to remember and celebrate someone or something.

illegal – against the law.

slave – a person owned by someone else.

Index

Online Resources

popbooksonline.com

Thanks for reading this Cody Koala book!

Scan this code* and others like it in this book, or visit the website below to make this book pop!

popbooksonline.com/presidents-day

*Scanning QR codes requires a web-enabled smart device with a QR code reader app and a camera.